Aztec History

A Captivating Guide to the Aztec Empire, Mythology, and Civilization

Free Bonus from Captivating History (Available for a Limited time)

Hi History Lovers!

Now you have a chance to join our exclusive history list so you can get your first history ebook for free as well as discounts and a potential to get more history books for free! Simply visit the link below to join.

Captivatinghistory.com/ebook

Also, make sure to follow us on:

Twitter: @Captivhistory

Facebook: Captivating History:@captivatinghistory

Contents

Introduction

For many years, the Aztecs have captured our imaginations. Stories from the original European invaders combined with unique, awe-inspiring ruins and legends that speak of palaces of gold create an image of Aztec society defined by grandeur, wealth, and splendor. But who exactly were the Aztecs? Where did they come from? How did they rise to control such a wide expanse of land? And if they were so powerful, how was it possible for them to fall from power and dominance just three years after contact was first made with the Spaniards?

Luckily for us, we can answer most of these questions. Detailed historical accounts from Spanish conquistadors, Aztec documents such as the Codex Mendoza (a detailed account of Aztec rulers, the tribute system and daily life in the empire created in the mid-15th century after Spanish conquest,, and a wealth of archaeological sites make it possible to uncover some of the secrets of this ancient civilization.

In truth, the daily life of an Aztec commoner was not all that different from the life of today's common folk. Sure, technology was far more primitive, and there was a constant looming threat of complete and total destruction at the hands of one of the many Aztec gods. But apart from this, the average Aztec citizen was responsible for working their land, paying taxes, and providing for their families. When they weren't doing this, they were either off fulfilling their obligatory military service or perhaps enjoying a relaxing game of *patolli* with their friends.

While the life of a commoner in the Aztec empire seems okay, it was one full of hard work and uncertainty about the future. Few Aztec commoners were able to enjoy goods or services beyond the basic necessities for life and worship. Aztec leaders, on the other hand, lived a life of luxury. Servants, concubines, and laborers were bound to the nobility, and this life of luxury helped employ the ever-growing Aztec population.

Overall, the Aztec Empire, or the empire of the Triple Alliance, would grow in both size and population to be one of the largest in the ancient world. It was the second largest empire in all of America in the 16th century; only the Incas occupied more territory. At its peak, the Aztec Empire included some 50 or more city-states and upwards of 3 million people. However, this would nearly all disappear with the arrival of the Spanish. Superior weapons and devastating disease laid waste to much of what the Aztecs had built over the previous centuries.

Many of the secrets of the Aztec Empire have been uncovered. Yet many more still remain. Historians and archaeologists are constantly learning more about the way the Aztecs lived, how they organized themselves politically, and how they interpreted their position in the world and the cosmos.

This guide will review some of the major parts of Aztec history, including a detailed account of who the Aztecs were, how they expanded, how they lived, how they worshiped, how they played, and finally, how they died. By taking the time to remember the Aztecs and their accomplishments, we can all play a part in making sure one of the world's greatest civilizations lives on forever.

Chapter 1 –Where Did the Aztecs Live?

To understand Aztec civilization, it's important to grasp the diverse geographical landscape in which their empire thrived. The Aztecs are considered a Mesoamerican civilization, with Mesoamerica being the term to describe the area extending from North-Central Mexico to the Pacific Coast of Costa Rica.

As you would expect from an area so large, the defining characteristic of Mesoamerican geography is diversity. Coastal lowlands differ greatly from central highlands in all aspects, from climate, soil conditions, and availability of crops. It's important to note that what is traditionally considered the Aztec Empire, the area surrounding Tenochtitlán (present-day Mexico City) in the Valley of Mexico, differed greatly from its surrounding territories and relied on them for a number of different essential and luxury resources.

In general, Mesoamerica can be divided into three major environmental zones. The tropical lowlands refer to the lands lying below 1,000 meters (~3280 ft). These parts of Mesoamerica are referred to as *tierra caliente* (hot lands). All of Mesoamerica lies in a tropical climate, but higher elevations bring temperatures down. Near the coasts, however, this does not happen. Temperatures are hot, the air is humid, and rainfall is heavy. The principal landscapes in this zone are heavy-vegetation forests or savanna grasslands. The Aztecs relied on these territories for such goods as colorful feathers from parrots and quetzals (used for rituals and art), jaguar skins, tobacco, and jade.

As one moves inland, they enter the Mesoamerican Highlands. The highlands refer to areas that are between 1,000-2,000 m (~3280-6560 ft.) and are often referred to as *tierra templada* (temperate country). Temperatures hover around 70°F (21°C), and with distinct dry (January to May) and rainy (June to October) seasons, rainfall is sufficient in most parts of the Mesoamerican Highlands for people to successfully grow crops year-round.

While this territory is mountainous, human civilization has flourished in river valleys and other expanses with relatively flat land. Many other Mesoamerican civilizations found their home here, including the Mixtecs, Zapotecs, Tarascans, and highland Maya. The southern part of the heart of the Aztec Empire falls in this territory.

If you continue climbing up the mountains and towards the center of present-day Mexico, you enter the Central Mexican Plateau. Everywhere you go is at least 2,000 m (~6560 ft.) above sea level, which brings tropical temperatures way down and gives the plateau the name *tierra fría* (cold lands). The heart of the Aztec civilization was in the center of this plateau, the Valley of Mexico. But additional large valleys lie to the north, west, and east. Rainfall varies widely across this part of Mesoamerica, and cooler temperatures make frost a challenge for farmers, shortening the growing season and the overall availability of crops.

In the heart of the Valley of Mexico is Tenochtitlán, the Aztec capital. Built essentially on Lake Texcoco, Tenochtitlán was founded in 1325 and would grow to be a powerful city, the largest in Mesoamerica. Agreements with nearby city-states greatly expanded their capacity to grow and expand in both territorial and cultural influence.

Surrounding the Valley of Mexico, the elevation drops rapidly, and cultural diversity expands. To the north, Otomi-speakers dominated and remained relatively outside Aztec influence. To the west is the Toluca Valley, where Aztec-Nahuatl speakers shared territory with many different language groups. And to the east is the Puebla Valley, where several cities in the northern part of this territory resisted Aztec conquest and remained independent until the Spaniards arrived in 1519.

It's important to grasp the environment in which the Aztec Empire developed. Challenging terrain and cultural diversity made for a state of constant jockeying for power and influence. Establishing dominance in this area required a wise and efficient use of resources, along with a good deal of force and cunning, and the making of enemies along the way. This would be the eventual demise of the Aztec Empire, but it first facilitated a civilization that is responsible for much of Mesoamerican history.

Chapter 2 –Who Were the Aztecs?

The first thing to remember is that the Aztecs are the Aztecs only to us. This is the name historians use to describe the empire formed by the Nahuatl-speaking peoples who referred to themselves as the Mexica. The name Aztec is said to derive from the word Atzlan, which describes a place in Northern Mexico where it's believed the semi-nomadic Mexica originated. The exact location of Aztlan is unknown, though it is generally agreed to be in the north of modern Mexico. Many Nahuatl-speaking tribes claim their origin to be from Atzlan, but even the Aztecs we know did not have a clear idea of where it is. Montezuma I famously sent out a band of warriors and explorers to find it, but they were unsuccessful. The word Aztec comes from *Aztecah,* which means "people from Aztlan." However, this name was not used by the Aztecs to describe themselves. It became the accepted term over time. In general, it's unclear if the Aztecs move to the Valley of Mexico was by design or rather as part of a much larger southern migration carried out by the people of Northern Mexico.

The Aztecs were likely related in some form or another to the Toltecs, a civilization that grew to prominence in Northern Mexico in the 11th and 12th centuries. It was very important for early Aztec rulers to establish some sort of lineage with the Toltecs, as they felt this provided them with legitimacy. Additionally, the Aztecs would adopt and adapt many of the religious and spiritual practices of the Toltecs. For example, the Aztec god Quetzalcóatl, who is considered to be one of the most important gods in the Aztec religion, was the priest-king of Tula, the Toltec capital.

However, despite efforts by Aztec rulers to make direct connections to the Toltecs, it's far more likely that the people we now refer to as Aztecs were actually a combination of different hunter-gatherer tribes. It's unclear why, by early Aztec sovereigns found it necessary to legitimize their rule by claiming lineage with the Toltecs. As the empire grew and consolidated, this became less important. Yet some of the cultural and religious similarities are hard to ignore. However, in the end, it was the Nahuatl language that brought distinct cultural groups together to form what we now know as the Aztecs.

The Aztec Empire typically refers to what is known as the Triple Alliance. This was an alliance between the three cities in the Valley of Mexico, Tenochtitlán, Texcoco, and Tlacopan. The capital was to be Tenochtitlán, and it would grow to be the center of Aztec influence in the region.

The story, or stories, of the founding of Tenochtitlán sheds some light into Aztec values and worldviews that can be seen throughout the empire's history. The first story speaks to the power of religion and myth. After having been forced to settle elsewhere, the god Uitzilopochtli came to the priest Quauhcoatl and told him they should build their city where they find a *tenochtli* cactus with an eagle sitting on top. Legend has it the men with whom Quahcoatl was traveling found this cactus shortly thereafter and chose to settle there.

Another story explains why the Mexica were looking for a new place to settle. They were semi-nomadic, meaning they changed lands according to agricultural or pastoral needs. Forced to the south, they found most of the Valley of Mexico already occupied by other tribes and linguistic groups.

The first Mexica settlement, Chapultepec, was on a hill on the western shore of Lake Texcoco. Founded in roughly 1250, Chapultepec would not last long. By the end of the 13th century, the Tepanecs of Azcapotzalco, the tribe that had established dominance in the area surrounding Chapultepec, had driven the Mexica from Chapultepec and gave them permission to live on the barren lands surrounding the city-state of Tizapan, also in the area surrounding Lake Texcoco.

In 1323 though, the Mexica played a cruel trick on their new ruler. After asking for his daughter's hand in marriage, they promptly sacrificed her and flayed her skin. A priest then presented himself to the king wearing his daughter's skin. Horrified, this caused the Mexica to be expelled from Tizapan. They were once again forced to find a new place to live.

It's impossible to know if the Aztecs chose Tenochtitlán because of divine intervention or out of necessity. Forced to evacuate two prior settlements, the Mexica could no longer be too picky. Tenochtitlán is essentially a swamp, and its growth was due in large part to the tremendous effort of adding dirt and mud to build solid ground upon which a city could be built.

No matter the reason, Tenochtitlán was the center of what we now refer to as the Aztec Empire. Its symbol is, fittingly, an eagle perched upon a cactus. This image appears in the center of modern-Mexico's flag, indicating the role this ancient civilization plays in the collective psyche of one of the world's largest modern nations.

It's becoming increasingly common to refer to Tenochtitlán by its full name: Mexico-Tenochtitlán. The exact meaning of the name is not fully understood. Tenochtitlán clearly draws its moniker from the Nahuatl word for prickly pear, *tenochtli*, but the origin of the word *Mexico* is more difficult to uncover. Most scholars now agree it means "in the center of the moon," with the moon referring in this context to Lake Texcoco. This deduction is confirmed when looking at the how the name Mexico-Tenochtitlán is translated into the nearby Otomi language, where the Mexican capital is referred to as "anbondo amedetzana." Bondo is known to mean prickly pear, and amedetzana means "in the middle of the moon." Many sources and historical documents will refer to the city as simply Tenochtitlán, but those living during the height of the Aztec empire would have used its full name.

These origin stories of Mexico-Tenochtitlán reflect how we would eventually come to perceive this ancient civilization and culture. Aztec mythology and religion has been heavily studied, and most modern depictions of Aztec life include at least some reference to the brutality of human sacrifice. Images of priests ripping out the beating hearts of citizens are aplenty. And while this did occur, Aztec culture was, as you would expect, decidedly diverse and dynamic, especially for a civilization of this size.

Estimates indicate more than 1 million people were living in the Valley of Mexico when Cortés came onto the scene in 1519. And there were likely another two or three million in the highlands surrounding it. These figures make the Aztec civilization the largest in the Americas at the time of European arrival.

It's also important to remember that when we talk about the Aztec Empire, we are in many ways talking about the period of time after the formation of the Triple Alliance. This was an agreement to unite the three major city-states surrounding Lake Texcoco, specifically Mexico-Tenochtitlán, Texcoco, and Tlacopan, and to place Mexico-Tenochtitlán at the center as the capital. The three cities would share bounties from trade and tribute, allowing them to orchestrate their expansion into the surrounding valley.

Chapter 3 – Government, City-States, and Expansion

Aztec civilization can be divided into two main periods: the Early Aztec period and the Late Aztec period. Many of the city-states that would become a part of the Aztec Empire were founded at the beginning of the 12ᵗʰ century. Most would persist and grow throughout the coming centuries, and many would become important city-states in the empire. However, as these towns grew into cities and eventually city-states, much of what had been constructed in the Early Aztec period was destroyed, leaving little archaeological evidence of these settlements.

The beginning of the Late Aztec period is usually associated with the founding of Mexico-Tenochtitlán in 1325. When the Mexica arrived, there was very little land that had not already been settled. Different tribes and ethnic groups occupied the territory, but over time, many of them would assimilate into Aztec culture. The only ethnic group able to maintain its own independent identity was the Otomi, who maintained their own linguistic and cultural traditions despite constant pressure from their Nahuatl-speaking neighbors.

The political system of the Aztecs was despotism. Kings and quasi-kings ruled over city-states and they interacted with other city-states in various ways. Sometimes they cooperated with each other, typically through trade and military alliances, but they also fought each other constantly. As such, relationships between city-states were ever-changing and unpredictable.

Nevertheless, the Aztec Empire is really best understood as a political alliance between some fifty or more city-states that occupied the Valley of Mexico. The only real political institution that bound them together was the system of taxes and tributes that was designed to help raise the status of sovereigns and the nobility and also to suppress and subdue the commoners. As the empire expanded, this tribute system became more demanding. And in cases where city-states fell under the control of the Aztecs because of military conquest, tributes were even harsher.

The golden age of the Aztec Empire began in 1428 with the formation of the Triple Alliance between Mexico-Tenochtitlán, Texcoco, and Tlacopan. This represents the most robust form of political cooperation between any of the city-states in the Valley of Mexico, and it was due to the economic and military might of these city-states that the Aztecs were able to eventually gain control over nearly all of the settlements in the Valley of Mexico and beyond.

This alliance, however, was born from war. Hostilities between the Mexica, or Aztecs, and the Tepanecs, a city-state that also had considerable influence in the Valley of Mexico, intensified around the year 1426. The Tepanecs tried to blockade Tenochtitlán in an effort to extract higher taxes and tributes. While attempting to intimidate the Mexica in Tenochtitlán, the Tepanecs, led by Maxtla, were also harassing the Acolhua in Texcoco. When they forced Netzahualcoyotl, the sovereign of Texcoco, to flee, the Mexica found an ally in their struggle against the Tepanecs. Furthermore, Motecuhzoma, the leader of Tenochtitlán at the time, was attempting to rally support for a rebellion in the Valley of Mexico by pandering to citizens of Tlacopan who were fed up with Tepanec rule and were looking for a change.

Total war broke out in 1428, and with the forces of Texcoco, Tlacopan, Tenochtitlán, and Huexotzinco combined, the Tepanecs were defeated, leaving the Mexica as the primary power in the Valley of Mexico. Being the largest and richest of the three city-states, and also having the largest military, Tenochtitlán was the natural choice for the center of this newly formed imperial alliance. The Huexotzinco, living on the other side of the mountains, were merely interested in removing the Tepanecs, but did not have any further ambitions in the Valley of Mexico. After the war's conclusion, they returned to their home and the remaining three city-states formed what we now call the Triple Alliance.

This collaboration was as much a military alliance as it was an economic cooperation. The first tenet was to agree not to wage war against each other and to support each other in wars of conquest and expansion. Taxes from these conquests would be shared, with two-fifths going to both Texcoco and Tenochtitlán and one-fifth to Tlacopan. The capital was to be in Tenochtitlán, meaning the leader of this city-state was the de facto emperor, yet this leader would be chosen somewhat democratically. An electoral college made up of nobles and dignitaries from all three city-states in the Alliance was responsible for choosing the leader of the pact. Itzcoatl was named the first emperor of the new Aztec Empire, even though Motecuhzoma had been the leader of Tenochtitlán. Motecuhzoma would have to wait his turn to assume the position of emperor.

After joining forces, the new Aztec Empire quickly set its sights on gaining control over the entire Valley of Mexico. Campaigns throughout the 1430s brought the cities of Chalco, Xochomilco, Cuitalhuac, and Coyocan under the influence of the Triple Alliance. After completing these conquests, the Aztecs looked further south, moving into the modern-day state of Morelos. Here they would conquer Cuauhnahuac (the modern-day city of Cuenravaca) and Huaxtepec. Located in lower elevations, the climates in these cities were much more favorable. Intensive agriculture produced impressive yields that the Aztecs desired so as to feed their people and enrich their empire.

In 1440, Itzcoatl died and Motecuhzoma I was chosen as the next emperor. The reign of Motecuhzoma I was an important part of Aztec history. He began construction on some of the more important Aztec temples, including the great temple of Tenochtitlán. But perhaps more importantly, Motecuhzoma I was responsible for consolidating political power into the hands of the Mexica.

As new city-states fell under the control of the Aztecs, Motecuhzoma I would install his own people as tax collectors to bypass the dynasties that had previously existed, centralizing power into the hands of Tenochtitlán and taking it away from competing tribes. Motecuhzoma I also established a new legal code that served to further distinguish the nobility from the common folk.

However, he was also interested in quelling rebellions and keeping city-states that had been conquered under his control. One thing he did to try and do was to create a new title, the quahpilli (eagle lord). Anyone could occupy this position and it was typically given to warriors who had been exceptionally successful in battle.

Motecuhzoma I also presided over one of the darker periods of the Aztec Empire. Severe drought hit the region in 1450, and this led to significant famines over the next four years. Thousands of Aztecs would die of hunger during this period. After the famines ended, there was a significant uptick in the amount of human sacrifices throughout the empire as it was widely believed that this drought and famine was the result of insufficient sacrifices in the years before 1450.

Motecuhzoma I and Nezahualcoyotl of Texcoco began a series of military campaigns in 1458 that would dramatically expand the sphere of Aztec influence in the region. They were able to extend their control well beyond the Valley of Mexico, establishing dominance throughout the majority of the modern-day states of Morelos and Oaxaca.

When Motecuhzoma I died in 1468, Axayacatl, the grandson of both Motecuhzoma I and Itzcoatl, took over the throne. Most of his 13-

year rule was spent consolidating or reconquering some of the territories already seized by previous rulers. Axayacatl was succeeded by his brother Tizoc in 1481. However, he was a weak ruler and a poor military leader. He died in 1486 and was replaced by another one of his brothers, Ahuitzotl. Some evidence suggests Tizoc may have been assassinated as those in the center of the empire saw Tizoc as a liability.

When Ahuitzotl took the throne, he began another period of military conquest that would significantly expand Aztec-controlled territory. Specifically, he conquered much of the Valley of Oaxaca and the Soconusco Coast of Southern Mexico. Although they were the farthest from the imperial center, these areas were significant as they were important source of goods such as cacao and feathers, both of which were used by the nobility as means of expressing their wealth and higher social standing.

The reign of Ahuitzotl represents the most prosperous period of the Aztec Empire. Not only did it expand considerably in terms of the territory it controlled, but Ahuitzotl was also able to consolidate power within the Triple Alliance. He replaced the title *tlataoni,* which means "one who speaks," and was the Aztec word for sovereign, with *huehuetlatoani*, which means "supreme king." The other city-states were consulted less about imperial matters who seemed to have little desire in trying to regain control from the leaders of Tenochtitlán. The city's great temple was completed during the time of Ahuitzotl, indicating that his rule also presided over a period of significant economic prosperity.

When Ahuitzotl died in 1502, he was replaced by Motecuhzoma Xocoyotzin, who is often referred to in the history books as Montezuma, or Montezuma II who is not to be confused with Motecuhzoma I.. Following the footsteps of previous emperors that assumed power after a period of significant imperial expansion, Montezuma's reign was largely defined by his attempts to consolidate power. But this time, there seemed to be a more pointed effort to consolidate power not only into the hands of the Triple

Alliance, but also into the hands of Montezuma's family. He essentially abolished the status of many nobles, replacing them with people closer to his immediate circle. In court, Montezuma ruled with terror, leading some scholars to indicate that Montezuma may have been taking steps towards creating an absolute monarchy in the Aztec Empire.

The Aztec Empire was at its peak during the reign of Montezuma. It had political, economic, social, and militaristic control over a vast expanse of land that was populated by some 3-4 million people. However, one particular failure of the previous rulers was their inability to successfully conquer the Tlaxcallans, a Nahuatl-speaking group that had made their home near the Valley of Mexico but who had resisted Aztec control.

The Aztec inability to conquer the Tlaxcallans proved to have disastrous consequences, as the Spanish were able to formed an alliance with them.

In fact, it was not hard at all for the Spanish to find support for their cause. To understand why this was the case, it's important to remember why the Aztecs were so concerned with expansion. They were looking for new city-states to subject to their tax and tribute system, and they were also looking to find new victims that could be sacrificed to the gods.

Furthermore, they were interested in expanding the empire's resource pool. A growing population meant increased demand for food. City-states at lower elevations were far more agriculturally productive, so conquest of these settlements made it easier for the Aztecs to feed their population, and it also represented an opportunity to enrich the Aztec elite through the collection of taxes and tributes. This strategy proved to be effective as the Aztec Empire grew in wealth and population considerably after the formation of the Triple Alliance, but it also had the effect of creating lots of animosity towards Tenochtitlán and the Aztec empire, something that would put the Aztecs at a significant disadvantage against the

Spaniards. There were plenty of people willing to sign up with the Spanish to help conquer the mighty Aztecs.

Throughout the 100 or so years of the Triple Alliance, the Aztecs took their civilization from a loose collection of semi-aligned but often warring city-states and turned it into the second largest empire in the New World (only the Incas controlled a wider expanse of territory) and the largest empire to ever have existed in Mesoamerica. Their system of expansion and consolidation was steady and directed. Emperors who succeeded in expanding territory were followed by leaders who managed to consolidate and organize the newly acquired lands and cities. Many setbacks occurred along the way—several cities were conquered, lost, and reconquered, for example—but in the grand scheme of things, the empire was growing in both size and influence at the time of Spanish arrival. However, contact with the Spanish would lead to the quick decline of what had become one of the most powerful empires of the ancient world.

Chapter 4 – The Arrival of the Spanish and the Decline of the Empire

With the landing of Christopher Columbus in the West Indies in 1492, the Spaniards were officially the first Europeans in the New World. Eager to explore, they set up a base in Cuba and began sending expeditions out to different parts of North, Central, and South America. One such expedition was that of Hernán Cortés. The Spaniards had heard about a great power in Central Mexico. Rumors of great riches combined with a desire to expand Spanish influence in the new world led Cortés to set his sights on the Valley of Mexico and the Aztec empire.

Cortés' expedition was initially sanctioned and half-funded by the Spanish crown, with Cortés himself putting up the rest of the money needed for the mission to take place. However, shortly before he set sail for Mexico, the Spanish crown rescinded its support, but Cortés sailed anyway. Several expeditions would be sent after Cortés in an effort to arrest him and bring him into custody.

In 1519, Cortés arrived on the coast of Mexico near the modern-day city of Veracruz with about 500 soldiers. They were greeted by messengers from Montezuma, who had heard of these strange men exploring the coast. Montezuma was cautious of them and also thought they might be gods. The Aztecs who greeted Cortés offered him gifts both as a way of forging peaceful relations, but also to confirm whether or not these people were in fact divine. When given the gold, the Spaniards reportedly went crazy, and this display of greed and lust convinced the Aztecs that the newcomers were in fact not descendants from the heavens.

Cortés began his march inland, making allies along the way. He had heard rumors that the Aztec armies could number in the thousands, and even though the Spaniards had better weapons, Cortés knew he would need more troops if he hoped to be successful in his conquest. Moving inland, Cortés first allied with the Totonacs. Then, they made their way towards Tlaxcalla, the powerful city-state that had resisted the control of the Triple Alliance. After an initial conflict, Cortés was able to convince the Tlaxcallans to join him on his journey inland towards Tenochtitlán. When Cortés finally made his way into Central Mexico, he had several thousand troops under his command.

Their first stop was in the holy city of Cholula. They were welcomed at first, but Cortés feared an ambush and massacred thousands of unarmed civilians. Hearing of this, Montezuma became increasingly suspicious of the Spaniards. Fearing Spanish intentions and the size of their force, he continued to send gifts as a way of trying to win Spanish friendship and discourage hostility, but all this did was increase the desire Cortés and his men had of reaching and conquering the Aztecs. Montezuma kept sending gold, and it was gold that the Spaniards wanted.

When the Spaniards arrived, Montezuma welcomed them by putting them up in what was the equivalent of a royal palace. Cortés responded by taking Montezuma prisoner. He then began to rule Tenochtitlán, pretending that he was acting under the guidance of the Aztec emperor. In 1520, Cortés received word from his scouts that an expedition had been sent to Mexico to arrest him, so he left Tenochtitlán with half of his forces to fight this expedition. He was successful and then returned to Tenochtitlán to finish the job of bringing the Aztecs under Spanish control.

Upon returning to the Aztec capital, Cortés found that tensions had arisen which put the Spaniards in great danger. They made plans to flee the city and regroup, but when trying to escape in the middle of the night, they suffered heavy casualties. Many Spaniards had loaded themselves with gold, which slowed them down and made them easier targets. Eventually, the Spanish succeeded in escaping Tenochtitlán. They retreated to Tlaxcala in the mountains.

In the coming months, Cortés was able to regroup considerably. He marched again on Tenochtitlán with some 700 Spanish soldiers and around 70,000 native troops. They would then lay siege to the city for months. Diseases such as smallpox wreaked havoc on the city, decimating its population, and the Spanish cut off all sources of fresh water and stopped all shipments of food. Eventually, on August 13, 1521, Cuauhtemoc, who had replaced Montezuma as emperor, was captured, and the Spaniards claimed victory. A once great civilization would enter a dark period. The Spaniards, eager to exploit the people and the land for all they could, killed thousands of Aztecs and enslaved many more. The Aztec Empire, after nearly a hundred years of glory in the Valley of Mexico, was finished.

Many people unfamiliar with the way in which the Aztec Empire fell express surprise that such a small party of Spanish soldiers was able to topple such an immensely powerful empire. But this represents a severe misunderstanding of how Cortés was eventually able to conquer the Aztecs. First, his force was much larger than just a few hundred people. Long-standing rivalries combined with resentment towards the taxes and tributes imposed by the Aztecs meant it was very easy for Cortés to recruit allies in the fight to take down Tenochtitlán.

But the Spaniards had another weapon at their disposal, disease. Illnesses such as smallpox had never before been seen in Mesoamerica. While Europeans had been exposed to it for centuries and had developed immunities, the Aztecs had not. Hundreds of thousands would die of smallpox, the measles, the mumps, influenza, and many other diseases. This silent weapon proved to be one of the biggest reasons why the Spaniards were able to seize control over such a powerful empire in such a short period of time.

The story of the Aztec fall from dominance does not do justice to the impressive nature of their empire. They established one of the largest empires not only in the Americas but in the entirety of the ancient world. However, in the end, they were no match for European disease and firepower, and their dominance over the Valley of Mexico came to a screeching halt just a few short years after Cortés and the Spaniards landed on the Mexican peninsula.

Chapter 5 –A Day in the Life of an Aztec Citizen

Social classes and hierarchy dramatically influenced the life of the Aztec citizen. Rights, duties, and privileges were all determined as a result of one's social standing. Nobles, possessing more resources and ability to mobilize them, had the greatest amount of agency and autonomy. However, when taking a closer look at the lives of the most distinct classes, it is clear that upward mobility was indeed possible. Not even a slave was destined to be a slave for his or her entire life, and achieving freedom was not all too difficult, especially when compared to the slavery that would emerge in the European colonies.

Nonetheless, analyzing daily life in Aztec society according to class paints a useful picture as to how people viewed their lives and how they decided to live them. Nobles were largely responsible for tasks such as running the government, owning land, and commanding the army. Commoners were far more numerous than nobles, and they were relied upon to support the nobility with food and other goods. The success of Aztec expansion is due in large part to this balance. A productive and content working class supported a nobility that recognized its power depended upon being attentive to the needs of the commoners.

The Sovereign, the Dignitaries, and the Nobles

The ruling classes of Aztec society can be crudely stratified into three groups. At the top was the sovereign, given the title of *tlatoani* Each city-state had its own *tlatoani* With the formation of the Triple Alliance, the title huehuetlatoani was introduced to refer to the leader of the pact. The term *tlatoani* can be used to describe the head of a city-state, and also the head of the Aztec empire, depending on the context in which it is written.

Below the sovereign were the dignitaries, usually close relatives or friends of the sovereign. And underneath the dignitaries were the nobility, or the *pilli*. These three groups were responsible for the administrative, bureaucratic, and gubernatorial duties of the empire. In the early days of Aztec civilization, this group was small, but it would grow considerably over the centuries, expanding its influence over the affairs of the empire.

The Sovereign

The title *tlataoni* translates into "the one who speaks," and it can be understood to mean emperor. Although the first *tlatoanis* attempted to establish lineage with the Toltecs and the gods, most emperors were elected. While *Ttlataoni* was the title given to the sovereign of the Aztec Empire, it was also the name for high-ranked dignitaries who ruled a city-state and its surrounding area.

It's important to remember that the Aztec Empire wasn't an empire in the traditional sense. It did not have one designated leader who passed power down through his lineage. Instead, the Aztec power was derived from the Triple Alliance. As a result, it's possible to find the word *tlataoni* in reference to the leaders of one specific city-state and also to the heads of Mexico-Tenochtitlán, who, since they resided in the empire's capital, are considered to be the heads of the larger Aztec "nation."

Each city-state had its own set of rules for the succession of leaders. Some followed strict ancestral lines, being careful to emphasize their relation from one particular tribe or another in an attempt to attribute their claim to rule to the gods. However, many city-states chose new leaders by voting after the previous *tlataoni* had died. This is a tradition that traces its roots back to the early days of Aztec life in the Valley of Mexico. The *tlataoni* that was chosen to rule Mexico-Tenochtitlán and the Aztec Empire as a whole was always elected, although as the empire expanded, the group of people responsible for this vote would shrink significantly.

In the beginning, when the Aztecs first settled in the Valley of Mexico, voting took place across the city, with most adult males having the chance to cast their vote for who the leader should be. However, as the empire expanded and it became impossible to gather everyone for a vote, an electoral college comprised of dignitaries emerged to elect the emperor. So, as the empire expanded, the power to elect the next *tlatoani* drifted further and further from the people. In fact, by the time the Spanish arrived at the beginning of the 16th century, the group of people responsible for choosing the empire's leader was around 100. Considering the population of the Aztec Empire at the time of Spanish arrival was in the millions, it's clear that power and government in Aztec slowly consolidated into the hands of a small oligarchy that came from the upper echelons of society.

After taking command, the sovereign had three main roles: commander in chief, representative of the ruling class and enforcer of the rule of law, and protector of the common people. In our traditional understanding of government structures, the Aztec Empire was a monarchy. However, as mentioned earlier, it combined some aspects of democracy, namely the election of the head of state as well as the individual right to vote. The slow degradation of these characteristics over time eroded the Aztec claim to democracy, but it's still important to recognize its presence.

The name *tlatoani* was no mistake. "The one who speaks" fits the Aztec emperor because of the expectation that this individual would be able to command authority in council through long, eloquent speeches designed to sway the opinions and perspectives of the cabinet members. It was in these sessions that the emperor and his council would debate the future of the Aztecs.

The other title of the emperor, *tlacatecuhtli*, is directly derived from the emperor's responsibility as commander in chief of the military. *Tlacatecuhtli* literally translates into "chief of the warriors." A good deal of the emperor's time was spent conducting various military campaigns. Since the three cities of the Triple Alliance were all powerful city-states in their own right, the Aztec sovereign had a considerable force at his disposal to command as he saw fit.

The last major responsibility of the Aztec sovereign was to the people. While Aztec leaders did not formally proclaim a divine right to rule, the voting process, combined with the coronation ceremonies, instilled the idea that the sovereign had been chosen not by the people or the nobility but rather by the gods, specifically Tezcatlipoca, who is known for having great wisdom due to a magic mirror that allows him to see all at all times.

Defending the temple of Uitzilopochtli was one of the primary responsibilities of any Aztec sovereign, in addition to ensuring all the gods received their due worship. After tending to their duties to the gods, Aztec rulers were then responsible to the people.

The Aztec sovereign is traditionally seen as both the "father and mother of Mexico." He is responsible for caring for the people, for helping fend off famine, and for warding off drunkenness and other unwanted behaviors in the cities and towns.

Most scholars of Aztec documents indicate that rulers took this responsibility seriously. There appears to have been a real affinity between the rulers and the ruled. Despite attributing their ascension to the throne to divine intervention, all records point to the fact that rulers still did not consider themselves to be above or higher than their subjects. And there are lots of examples of rulers acting in a truly benevolent manner. For example, Motecuhzoma I is famous for having doled out some 200,000 loads of clothes and maize to people from Auitzol so that they could recover from a great flood.

As with most things in the Aztec Empire, it's important to remember the depiction of the sovereign changes as you move throughout the territory. This close bond between ruler and ruled was one felt mostly in the center of the empire, mainly in Mexico-Tenochtitlán and the surrounding Valley of Mexico. This connection between sovereign and subject was much weaker in provincial territories. Tributes and taxes were felt more harshly and the benefits of these were distributed more narrowly, leaving provincial settlements with a much different understanding of their sovereign than their metropolitan counterparts.

The Dignitaries

Directly below the sovereign in the Aztec social hierarchy are the dignitaries. These individuals were typically the close relatives or friends of the *tlataoni*, and they were responsible for carrying out many of the decisions of the sovereign.

The exact title for each dignitary and their corresponding duties varied greatly from city-state to city-state and from *tlataoni* to *tlataoni*. Each position was filled according to the needs of that particular city. Or, positions were created to give titles and status to the people in the *tlataoni's* inner circle. who were considered significant enough to deserve a position in the court.

The duties of these individuals ranged anywhere from the protection of a temple to the management of granaries and other facilities where taxes and tributes were stored. The diverse names for all the different titles are too great to possibly list. From these dignitaries, the *tlataoni* would choose his council. This small group was responsible for advising the *tlataoni* on all important issues regarding the administration of the state. They were to be consulted before each and every military campaign and their blessing was needed before beginning something new.

Additionally, these individuals often made up part if not all of the electoral college that would be responsible for choosing the next emperor. This represents a stark change from the way leaders were chosen when the Aztecs first settled in the Valley of Mexico. By the time the Spanish arrived, the Aztec state was no longer a democracy but instead an oligarchy protected by a powerful emperor. The main effect of this was to further stratify society. While upwards mobility was possible—a member of the working class could be recruited into the nobles if it proved favorable for the nobility to do so— it was not common.

Somewhere around the time of Motecuhzoma I (early 15th century), the title of *Ciuacoatl* enters into the records of Aztec history. Curiously translated to "woman-serpent," the *Ciuacoatl* was essentially the vice-emperor. He was responsible for carrying out the rule of law, primarily by being the supreme judge in martial and criminal law. He would hear cases and make judgments on appeals, decide which warriors would be rewarded, organize military campaigns, manage imperial finances, organize the electoral college after the emperor's death, and serve as head of state while the election process took place.   This individual wielded great responsibility in Aztec administration. Being chosen for this position was considered one of the highest honors a *tlataoni* could bestow upon an individual.

Nobles

The next layer of the ruling class is the nobility, or the *pipiltin* or *pilli* (sing.). Together with the sovereign and the dignitary, the nobility comprised only about 5 percent of the total Aztec population, but they were the ones in charge. The *pipiltin* were not as involved in the running of the entire empire as the dignitaries and the sovereign were. Instead, their responsibility was in managing the territory that had been given to them and in maintaining their palace.

It's clear that the *pipiltin* saw working-class commoners as their subjects, and they considered the primary purpose of the commoner's life to be service to the nobility. There was no uniform level of treatment, though, among the nobility. Depending on the individual in charge and the circumstances of their position, living conditions of the commoners could range from barely burdensome to borderline slavery.

Regardless of the way the *pili* treated his subjects, the common folk were bound to their local lord, and they were responsible for furnishing certain goods for him and also for working his land. Furthermore, since the Aztecs had no standing army, each commoner, specifically the men, was expected and required to serve when a military campaign was launched. Unfortunately, there exists little in the form of numerical or anecdotal data to help uncover the full extent of the duties required of commoners to their respective lords.

One of the defining characteristics of the nobility was their palaces. It was very important that the *pipiltin* found ways to distinguish themselves from the commoners and one of the ways to do this was to build a large, luxurious home, typically on some of the best farmland in the region. Even in small, provincial towns, the local noble would build a large home using the finest materials available. Since many nobles were polygamists, they would often build homes with separate apartments inside for each one of their families.

However, it should never be forgotten that the nobility relied on the commoners to maintain their position of privilege. Each commoner was expected to pay taxes or duties to their respective noble, and the nobles relied upon the commoners to work their land and help produce goods that they could sell and use to maintain their position of prestige in society.

When looking at the way the nobility interacted with the commoners, it's easy to see how Aztec society was rather unequal. The nobility was aware of this, and since maintaining their elevated social position was one of their primary goals, they undertook a series of activities that helped to fortify themselves as the protectors of society who deserved the special treatment they received.

The first way in which the nobility kept people satisfied with the stratified nature of Aztec society was through ideas. By influencing what was spoken about at the temples and by controlling the rhetoric among the people, Aztec nobility was able to entrench in people ideas such as "everyone has duties to perform," "suffering and hard work is the natural state of human existence," and "human fate is in the hands of the gods." These messages helped quell any movements from below to challenge the authority of the nobility.

However, they needed something else to stand behind these words and ideas to make them more powerful and influential. Coercion defined much of the interaction between the nobility and the commoners. Many commoners would come under the rule of a noble as a result of conquest. The punishment for not paying tribute/taxes or for not working the noble's land was a return to conflict. And since the Aztecs had already proved their dominance, this particular path did not offer much promise to the conquered people. As such, it was a far better alternative to simply submit to the new political order than to bother trying to do anything to change it.

The third way in which the nobility separated themselves from the commoners and thus maintained their superior position was material consumption. Nobles were known for wearing the most expensive clothing, eating the most exotic foods, and living in the most elaborate houses. Special rules were also set up to help maintain this segregation. Nobility was only allowed to marry within the nobility, and they were expected to support each other in times of crises.

There was of course a need to ensure that commoners had enough food to eat and shelters to live in. But beyond that, and particularly as one travels further and further from the large city-states in the Valley of Mexico, there was little effort made by the nobility to improve the lives of the commoner. The commoners were the subjects, and they were expected to serve in whichever way made the most sense for the lord and the empire.

Commoners

The life of a commoner in Aztec civilization was dedicated nearly entirely to work. From the moment of birth, gender roles were ascribed to a child; men were expected to grow up to be warriors and to work in the same occupation as their father, and girls were to tend to the household by cooking, cleaning, weaving, and having children.

Because an Aztec commoner was expected to work, they are introduced to this way of life from a young age. Evidence from the Codex Mendoza, one of the most significant primary sources from the time, indicates that by the age of five boys were already carrying firewood and other goods to the nearby marketplaces and girls had already been taught to hold a spindle and spin. At the age of seven, boys were catching fish and girls were spinning cotton.

These demands were enforced on children through a system of threats and punishment. Aztec children were instructed by their parents to not be idle, as this would bring about bad behavior. To give an example, 8-year-old children who were caught being deceitful to their father would be pierced in the body with spikes. Older children were beaten with sticks if they were rebellious. Until the age of 15, children were taught primarily in the home by their parents; after this age they would head off to school for further training according to their gender and the relevant roles they would need to fill.

As with nearly everything in ancient Aztec society, school was divided by class. The school for commoners, known as the *telpochalli*, were established to teach children singing, dancing, and musical instruments (for use in rituals). Most boys would also receive military training. Service was mandatory for all men, so upon completing their training, most men would enter the army and be sent off to support the empire's expansionist strategy. The nobility were educated in the calmecac, where they were taught more advanced subjects such as religion, writing, mathematics, etc.

Marriage was also a critical part of growing up. Typically, pairs were made by parents or other elders, and by the age of 12, most Aztecs were married. From then on, gender roles became even more pronounced. Men were expected to work outside the home, typically in farming. When the seasons changed and agricultural activity slowed down, most Aztec men would be sent away from home. Military service was obligatory as was labor. If men weren't sent away to war, they were sent elsewhere to farm, likely to the land of a noble, as these people were exempt from both military and labor service.

Aztec women spent most of their time in the home cooking and preparing food. She was also responsible for cleaning the home, something considered to be more of a ritual than a chore, and also for burning incense and maintaining the home's altar. As such, women played a more significant role than men inside the home.

While duties and obligations occupied most of the time of an Aztec commoner, this did not entirely predestine their life. There were ample opportunities for a commoner to advance themselves and even possibly join the nobility. Aztec society was set up to receive this kind of movement between classes. One of the primary reasons for this was the way in which land ownership was structured in Aztec society.

Technically speaking, land could not be owned individually. Instead, it was collectively owned under the management of the *calpulli*, the chief. Each man was given individual rights to work a piece of land. They were free to work it as they pleased, but they were required to pay taxes and tribute on the bounty they received from the land. In exchange they were allowed a vote for the *calpulli* and could benefit from public services offered by the *calpull,* such as nicer temples, access to fresh water from aqueducts, and security.

Arable land in the Valley of Mexico, however, was scarce. Most of the best land was that which had a shoreline with Lake Texcoco, and because of this, the vast majority of Aztec citizens lived an urban life, depending on the provinces to supply the cities with goods. This in turn created another distinction in Aztec society: provincial/urban. Both paid taxes, yet the urban Aztec stood in a much better position to benefit from these taxes, as most improvements were centered on urban areas.

While land use was a right of commoners, it did come with certain privileges and benefits, but these rights were not for free. The right to use land was accompanied by the expectation that it would be used. If more than two years passed and the land remained idle, the one granted rights to work it would be subjected to severe admonishment from the *calpulli* and the wider community. After several more years of inactivity, these land rights could be stripped away, dropping that man and his family into the landless class, which enjoyed fewer rights and privileges.

While this was a possibility, it rarely occurred. The commitment to production and the commoner's relative autonomy contributed to the growth of the Aztecs in Central Mexico, and they are a big reason why they became the dominant force of the region. However, as the Aztecs advanced, more and more, exceptions were made to the labor requirement. Less land and more workers meant not every person was needed to effectively work the land. It also helped generate wealth, which expanded the nobility, diversified urban Aztec life, and created further economic and social inequalities.

This stratification occurred largely through changes in the traditional understandings of land ownership and use. The idea of common ownership eroded over time, and nobility were known to take land and assume control over it, limiting the commoner's ability to amass wealth by themselves. This situation was intensified as a result of the tax and tribute system. The whole population of a city paid taxes to the empire, and since there was no money, this duty was paid in goods. The tribute demanded of each city or provincial area was determined by the needs of the nobility at the time as well as the availability of resources. Tribute ranged from cloth, cloaks, corn, and oils to parrot feathers and precious gems.

Although tribute was varied, it's clear it brought a great deal of wealth into Mexico-Tenochitlan, further strengthening the Aztec Empire. A good measure for wealth at the time is the *quatchtli*, which was the equivalent of 20 loads of cloth. One *quatchtli* was considered the equivalent of a year's worth of living. At the peak of tribute gathering in Mexico, some 100,000 *quatchili* were being brought into Mexico from city-states subjected to the Aztez tribute systems, meaning 100,000 yearly livings were accounted for in the capital through cloth tribute alone.

Part of the reason these tribute bounties grew so large is that they were established under hostile circumstances. Conquest was a major part of Aztec expansion, and upon establishing military dominance over a particular region, negotiations would commence between the victorious Aztecs and the conquered. Since the threat of renewed conflict always loomed large, the Aztecs usually found themselves in an advantageous position at the negotiating table, allowing them to place extravagant demands on newly-occupied territories and its citizens.

Military strength and a productive tribute system are the reasons the Aztec Empire was able to grow in both size and influence to become the dominant player in the region. But in many respects, it was one of the reasons why it would eventually fall. The gradual transition from a society where each individual was granted the rights to work a piece of land to one that was expected to produce large tributes for the central empire caused a great deal of resentment towards Mexico-Tenochtitlán and the Triple Alliance.

The mediocrity of daily life in tribal Mexico was slowly replaced. In its place came a life where most of a city or town's efforts were directed at satisfying the needs of dignitaries and the imperial elite. A longing for a return to the way things were led many provincial populations to support Cortés and the Spanish in their attempt to destroy the Aztec Empire, something that would play a pivotal role in the eventual European triumph.

As the empire expanded, however, a new class begin to emerge that would rest in between the nobility and the commoners: the merchants. As cities and towns became more connected, the demand for goods from afar, both for personal use and to meet tribute, expanded. Commoners who were able to successfully trade goods among towns became quite wealthy.

However, the irony of this is that this wealth remained largely undistributed. Unlike the nobility, sovereigns, and dignitaries who were expected to spend lavishly to uphold their social position, merchants were under no such pressure. They were free to save or spend their earnings in any way they saw fit. They certainly lived in much greater comfort and luxury than a commoner, but they were by no means as openly extravagant as those in the ruling class.

This merchant class would grow considerably in wealth, power, and influence as Aztec civilization advanced, but they would never pose any serious threat to the upper classes. And because the wealth accumulated by merchants was hardly distributed throughout the rest of the commoner class, they remained a relatively small group within Aztec society.

While it's true a commoner in 14th, 15th, and 16th century Mexico with their ability to freely work their own land had some degree of upward mobility, the more accurate reality is that the average person dedicated most of their life to labor and military service. Men would spend long periods of time away from home, and women were restricted to the household. This status quo was acceptable for some time, but as inequalities were created and deepened, resentment towards Mexico-Tenochtitlán and the Triple Alliance intensified, resulting in the breakdown of one of the largest civilizations not only in Mesoamerica but on all of the American continents.

Landless Peasants

In between the commoners and the lowest rank in Aztec society, the slaves, was yet another social class worth mentioning: the landless peasants. How one became landless is hard to discern, especially since it was part of Aztec custom that each person be granted a tract of land to work so that they could pay the necessary taxes and tributes required by the local lord. However, with warfare a near constant threat and with people being displaced as their towns and cities were conquered, this landless class did indeed grow as the empire advanced.

These individuals were essentially destined to a nomadic lifestyle; that is until they could find a noble willing to take them in. Nobles were nearly always looking for extra hands to work their often highly-productive land. A noble could take in a landless peasant and allow them to work in exchange for a rent, which was usually a portion of the goods they produced, or additional labor.

It is, however, important to note that being taken in by a noble did not bestow upon a landless peasant the same rights that others in the tribe had. For example, they were not allowed to vote in any of the town's elections. But there was some justice in this arrangement. Although he couldn't vote, the landless owed nothing to the town. He paid no taxes and was exempt from service and military obligations. Essentially, he was beholden only to the noble who had taken him in and given him a place to live and work.

Slaves

The lowest social class in Aztec society was, as is the case in nearly every civilization, the slaves. While the life of the slave was by no means comfortable and luxurious, it was far better than the forms of slavery that would come to the Americas with the formation of European colonies. In fact, accounts from the Spanish explorers and conquerors show the newcomers' surprise as to the rather benevolent treatment of slaves.

On the surface, Aztec slavery is very similar to other forms of slavery present throughout history. A slave belonged to one man and was obligated to complete the work given to him by that man. In exchange, he was clothed, housed, and fed. Men worked as farm-laborers or as servants, whereas women spun or wove clothing. Many female slaves also served as concubines to their masters.

However, beyond this, Aztec slavery begins to differ greatly from the version of slavery that would emerge after the Spanish arrived and conquered the Aztecs, which would be much harsher and much more punishing than anything that existed during Aztec times. One of the most shocking differences is that Aztec slaves were allowed to own goods, save money, buy land, and could even buy other slaves to help them work this land if they had the money to do so. A slave was also allowed to marry a free woman. It was a relatively common practice for a widow to marry one of her slaves, making this slave the head of the household. Any children they had would be born free, as would the children of two slaves. One could not be born into bondage.

And unlike what is often seen in other societies, the children of slaves were not ostracized from society. In fact, there was little to no stigma attached to being born from slave parents. Itzcoatl, one of the greatest emperors in Aztec history, was the son of a slave woman. This status in no way affected his ability to rise up the social ladder to assume a position of great status and responsibility.

Furthermore, slavery was not a perpetual state. There were several very realistic paths a slave could take to earn his or her freedom. For example, slaves were freed when their master died. They could not be passed onto another owner as part of an inheritance.

Slaves could be sold, but there existed a way for them to gain their freedom before being transferred to another owner. At the auction, they were free to run. No one except the master and the master's son could chase them. Should someone else chase after them, the punishment was enslavement. If the slave could escape and make it to the nearby palace or royal enclave, then they would be immediately granted their freedom. Emperors also had the chance to free slaves. Montezuma II, for example, was famous for emancipating large amounts of slaves while in power.

Slaves also had the opportunity to buy their own freedom. They could do this by returning to their master with the price he paid for them. Or, in some cases, they could earn their freedom by finding someone to take their place for them. Brothers and sisters were permitted to serve under the same master, and families were infrequently split. Often one of the harshest images of European slavery is of families being torn apart to be sold to different masters.

Of course, slavery is slavery, but in the Aztec Empire, it was a decidedly milder version of bondage that what is seen elsewhere throughout history, especially compared to what would come to the Valley of Mexico after the Spanish invasion, conquest, and colonization.

In Aztec society, a person could become a slave in a variety of different ways. Prisoners of war were typically sacrificed, but those who were not were usually sold into bondage. Some city-states required slaves as tribute and the towns paying such tribute would usually search outside the empire for people to turn over to the nobility.

Slavery was also a punishment for some crimes. The Aztec justice system did not deal with long punishments, choosing more immediate and often harsher punishments for certain crimes. For example, if a man was caught stealing, he would be forced to work as a slave to the institution or person he stole from for a period of time agreed to be equivalent to the value of whatever had been stolen. The only way he could avoid this forced labor would be to pay the noble or temple the full value of what it was he had stolen. Since few could do this, most thieves ended up in slavery at some point or another.

However, far and away the most significant reason a person would end up a slave in Aztec society was through personal choice. Drunks who could not maintain their land (or who were poised to have it taken from them as a result of it lying idle for too long), addicts of the game *patolli*, whores who no longer wished to remain in the profession, and debtors who could not pay up, among others, would routinely sacrifice their freedom as a way to ensure they could fill their stomachs and have a roof over their head.

It became common practice throughout the Aztec Empire for families to give up one of their sons as a slave as payment for a debt. When this son came of age and was able to be married off, the family would replace him with another son. This arrangement would continue until it was agreed that the debt had been paid. If the slave happened to die before the payment was completed, then the debt would be canceled. Slaves that were payment for debts were therefore often treated exceptionally well.

Another major difference between Aztec slavery and European slavery was that the selling of slaves was not common and was even tightly regulated. If a master was no longer capable of paying for all his slaves, then he could trade them. Oftentimes this would involve the slave himself going out and trying to find the best arrangement for his master, meaning it would not be uncommon to find slaves traveling independently through the countryside, something that is unheard of in other colonial slavery institutions. Slaves could also be sold when they were deemed to be idle or vicious. If the master could prove that he had given the slave three warnings to change his ways and if the slave still refused to work, then the master was allowed to put him in a wooden collar and bring him to the market to be sold. This was very uncommon, though, and only happened in the rarest of circumstances.

Furthermore, slaves were exempt from paying taxes or serving in the military. Their only duty was to their master, and if a slave was able to earn their freedom, then they were only beholden to themselves.

The nature of Aztec slavery speaks to the fluidity of Aztec society. While it's true that social classes stratified people into different groups according to wealth, power, and privilege, there was nothing really standing in the way of someone going from a slave all the way to the nobility. One could earn his or her freedom, associate with a town, work, and amass the wealth and influence needed to achieve a higher position in the empire. This, like all social mobility, was really the exception instead of the norm. And unsurprisingly, slavery became more prominent in the later periods of the Aztec Empire. As military conquest became more and more important, and as more and more tribes were forced under Aztec rule, the number of people put into bondage expanded. This type of social stratification, while useful in helping the empire grow, would eventually be one of the downfalls of the empire and is one of the reasons it was so vulnerable when Cortés and his expedition arrived at the Valley of Mexico in 1519.

Chapter 6 – Agriculture and Diet

To support the size and expanse of the Aztec Empire, which at the time of Spanish invasion totaled somewhere between 3-4 million people, agriculture needed to develop to be able to provide enough food for all these people.

As is the case in most Mesoamerican cultures, the Aztecs could not have risen to their eventual position of dominance =without *maize*, or corn. Maize is special for a variety of reasons. First, it can grow in a wide range of soil and climate conditions. Several varieties are known to have arisen throughout Mesoamerica that adapted specifically to the conditions of that region. Additionally, maize can be stored. In years of surplus, kennels can be left out to dry. Then, when they are needed, they can be soaked and consumed.

The next staple below maize in the Aztec diet was beans. Meat was not common in Mesoamerica, which has led some to question the nutritional health of the Aztecs. But a diet full of corn and beans can in fact supply the body with all 11 amino acids. This designation as a "complete protein" is what makes meat so important in the diet. But there are other ways of acquiring these nutrients, which the Aztecs seem to have been capable of doing on a large scale.

The essential food in Aztec culture, and in much of Mesoamerica today, is the tortilla. These are made by first soaking maize in an alkaline solution, usually water mixed with limestone. While this is done for flavor, it turns out this process is also helpful in releasing additional amino acids found inside corn that the body cannot get to on its own. After the corn has been soaked, it's then ground into a dough, formed into flat tortillas, and cooked in a clay oven. They can be consumed on the spot or later. This made tortillas an excellent option for men who needed to travel far for work or to fulfill their service to the nobility.

While maize and beans represent the bulk of the diet—they were eaten at nearly every meal—the Aztec diet was supplemented by fruits and vegetables, such as avocado, tomato, and nopal, the prickly pear cactus fruit. Chili peppers are frequently found in traditional Aztec foods, and they helped infuse Aztec people with vitamins A and C, as well as riboflavin and niacin.

Insects and worms were also important sources of protein. Other sources of protein came from plants. For example, when the Spanish arrived, they noted that Aztec women would collect spirulina algae from the lake and form it into cakes and breads. The foreigners looked down upon this food, but the Aztecs prized it for its protein content and also for its medicinal properties. Dogs, turkeys, and ducks were the only domesticated animals in the Aztec world, but they were infrequently used for meat. The flesh of larger animals such as cows or pigs was virtually nonexistent in the Aztec diet.

For these staple crops, fruits, and vegetables to be widely available throughout the empire, it was important that Aztec agriculture adapt to be able to meet the increased demand. In general, there are two different types of agriculture: extensive and intensive. Extensive agriculture is passive. Watering is done with nothing more than rain, little to no fertilizer is used, and farmers spend very little time weeding their plot. The advantage to extensive agriculture is that it requires very little human labor. But the main disadvantage is that it produces small yields. In the early Aztec era, extensive agriculture was sufficient, but as the population expanded, it became necessary to adopt more intensive forms of agriculture.

Intensive agriculture gets its name because it's the practice of intensively working a piece of land to be able to maximize its yield. The four main types of Aztec intensive agriculture were: irrigation, terracing, raised fields, and house-lot gardens.

Irrigation is the process of redirecting fresh water towards a field to help steady the flow of water and give the crops the chance to grow faster. In Central Mexico, where rainfall comes only during the rainy season, irrigation allowed the Aztecs to be able to extend the season and also to begin watering crops before the rains came in. This gave them a head start and allowed them to grow for longer, creating larger yields that could feed larger populations.

Irrigation was used wherever possible in Central Mexico. However, it was seen to a far greater degree in the area that occupies the present state of Morelos. This is significant because many of the cities in this area were the most advanced of the empire. Most scholars agree that widespread use of irrigation comes when there is a central authority capable of organizing labor and managing resources. By the time the Spanish arrived in the Valley of Mexico, the Aztecs had tapped into nearly every available fresh water source. Further intensification would have required additional coordination of both labor and resources from a central authority, which can help explain why the irrigated fields were consolidated in the more prosperous and bureaucratic parts of the empire.

Terracing was another important aspect of Aztec agriculture. Since the Valley of Mexico is a hilly, mountainous region, the places where land can be irrigated and cultivated intensively is rather limited. Terracing allowed cities and towns to make the most of their land by turning hills and mountains into arable lands. Most terracing was done with stone, but in some areas where slopes were less dramatic, Aztec farmers were able to use plants mashed together to form a mud-like solid.

Another hallmark of Aztec agriculture was raised fields. Many of the city-states that would come to be associated with the Aztecs lived in areas where swamps and marsh dominated the landscape. To make the most of this land, Aztec workers would dig a ditch near the swamp to drain the water. Then, they would carry in mud and muck from the swamp and fill it into the areas where the water had drained. This created a patch of solid land that could be farmed.

These fields are known as *chinampas*, and they are known for being quite productive. The mud and muck used to create the ground was organic material rich in all the nutrients needed to grow crops. And since these fields were built on top of a swamp, there was a constant supply of water. Furthermore, most of the swamps and marshes were in the southern part of the Valley of Mexico, which is warmer and at less risk for frost than many other parts of the valley. These three factors meant that *chinampas* became highly-productive components of the Aztec agricultural system. They also allowed for the diversification of crops since in most *chinampas* several crops could be planted each year.

The last type of intensive agriculture used in the Aztec era was house-lot gardening. This was the process of using the land on which a family lived to produce food and other goods. Most evidence from the period suggests this was a common practice for a typical Aztec citizen. Crops would be fertilized with organic material from the home, and family members would share the duties of weeding and harvesting. The productivity of these plots varied greatly depending on the size of the lot and the number of family members that were available to work it.

None of these methods of intensive agriculture were new to Mesoamerica. They had been used in some form or another for hundreds of years before the Aztecs. However, what was unique to the Aztecs was the extent to which these methods were used. The vast majority of the Valley of Mexico has been either irrigated or terraced at some point in time, and if one travels to the modern state of Morelos, there are still *chinampas* in use or on display for tourism.

In general, the Aztecs were successful in expanding agriculture to meet the needs of a population that exceeded three million, but had the Spanish not arrived; it's worth wondering how much longer they would have lasted. Arable land was scarce, and most of the fresh water was already in use. It's impossible to know "what if," but it's clear the Aztecs had all but tapped the capacity of the land they occupied.

Chapter 7 – Religion

Religion played a central role in the lives of Aztec leaders and citizens. Comprising a list of all the different ideologies and deities within Aztec religion, however, is essentially impossible. This is largely because there is no one Aztec religion. Instead, Aztecs combined a wide range of beliefs and ideas from other Mesoamerican cultures, specifically the Maya and the Toltec. However, there are some defining characteristics of Aztec religion that help shed some light on what life might have been like in 15th century Mexico.

Creation, Life, Death, and the Four Suns

The Aztecs believed that the Earth upon which we are currently living is in fact the fifth Earth to have existed. These Earths, or "suns," were created by the gods and ceased to exist on the day that had been predetermined according to the date in which they were created. Humans existed on each of these suns, but they were completely wiped out by catastrophe. This notion would come to define Aztec religion and also Aztec way of life. Essentially, it created the idea that life on Earth was in constant danger. If the current sun on which people lived was not given all its nourishment, then the Aztecs believed it may cease to exist and that they would be wiped out of existence just like when the previous suns were destroyed.

The first sun was named Nahui-Ocelotl, which translates to Four-Jaguar. This name was chosen because it was believed that on the first sun human beings were destroyed by jaguars. The second sun came to an end because of Nahui-Ehecatl, or Four-Wind. The belief was that a magical hurricane turned all the people on Earth into monkeys. The third sun, Nahui-quiahuitl, Four-Rain, ended as Tlaloc, the god of rain and thunder, unleashed a rain of fire on the Earth. Lastly, the fourth sun, Nahui-Atl, Four-Water, ended in a flood that lasted 52 years. It is said that only one man and one woman survived this flood, and they were promptly turned into dogs by the god Tezcatlipoca because they disobeyed his orders.

The fifth sun, which represents present humanity, was created by Quetzalcóatl, the Feather Serpent god. Legends speaks of Quetzalcóatl sprinkling his blood on the dried bones of the dead which in turn helped bring the bones to life and create humanity as we know it. This present sun is called Nagui-Ollin, or Four-Earthquake because it is supposedly doomed to disappear in a giant earthquake in which skeleton-esque monsters from the west, the *tzitzimime*, will come to kill all the people.

Aztecs believed two primordial beings were responsible for the creation of life and all living things, including the gods. They were Ometecuhtl, the Lord of the Duality, and Omeciuatl, the Lady of the Duality. This Earth exists between 13 heavens, which are above the Earth, and 9 hells, which are found below the surface of our world. These supreme creators live in the 13th heaven, and although they have largely withdrawn themselves from the management of the world, they are still responsible for all creation and death.

The descendants of the Lord and Lady of the Duality were the gods responsible for the creation of this Earth. The story in Aztec religion is that the gods had gathered at Teotihuacán in twilight, and one god threw himself into the fire as a sacrifice. When he emerged from the fire, he had been transformed into a sun. Yet he could not move. He needed blood to break his idleness, which the other gods willingly provided by sacrificing themselves. Life was essentially created from death, an ideology that would be at the center of Aztec religion and thought throughout their period of dominance in the Valley of Mexico.

The Aztec beliefs on life after death are rather bleak as compared to other cultures and religions. According to Aztec tradition, anyone who died of leprosy, dropsy, gout, or lung diseases was sent to the old paradise of the rain god Tlaloc because it was believed that he had been the reason for their death. Because of this special selection by one of the gods, the souls of these individuals were sent to paradise.

After that, there were two main categories of people that went up to the heavens with the sun when they died. These two categories were: warriors who had died in battle or who were sacrificed and the merchants who had been killed in faraway lands, and women who had died giving birth to her first child.

The rest of the people were sent to Mictlan, the land of the 9 hells that exists underneath the Earth. It is said that it took them four years to travel through all 9 hells, and once they finally got there, they would disappear altogether. Back on Earth, ancestors would give offerings 80 days after someone's death, and then at every anniversary of their death for the next four years. After the fourth year, the connection between the living and the dead was broken.

This version of reality is no doubt shocking for modern-day readers, but it helps to better understand the Aztecs and their way of life. Two important themes emerge from this creation story. The first is that the Aztecs believed that the world was in constant peril. Four worlds had been created before this one, and there is no reason to believe this world will not suffer the same fate.

The other key takeaway from the Aztec creation story is the importance of blood in keeping this world alive. Since the first god who threw himself in the fire was turned into a sun but could not move until he was given the blood of the other gods, Aztecs felt it was their primary duty to provide blood to the Earth so that it would continue moving and fend off its impending doom. And the Aztec version of what happens after life served to reinforce this idea. Nothing was waiting for them after death, so the only motivation for living was to provide blood for the continued existence of this Earth. This is the primary reason why human sacrifice became such an essential aspect of Aztec religion and way of life, and also why war was such an integral part to the running and managing of the Aztec Empire.

Human Sacrifice

Perhaps some of the more influential images of the Aztecs that has come out of Hollywood and other pop culture outlets is that of an Aztec priest, standing at the tip of one of their pyramid temples, holding the beating heart of a person who had just been sacrificed. This image does not reflect the totality of the Aztec Empire. But it would be a mistake to downplay just how important this practice was to the Aztecs and also how much of a role it played in the day-to-day decisions of nearly everyone in the empire, from sovereign to slave.

Since the fate of the Earth depended on people feeding it blood every day, the Aztecs believed life itself also required blood. To deny the Earth the blood it needed to survive would be to kill all the life that lived on Earth and eventually the Earth itself. Because of this perspective, sacrifice became an essential duty for nearly every Aztec.

Sacrifices took place in a variety of different ways. The most common was at a temple. The victim was stretched out on their back over a circular stone. This would leave their torso exposed to the skies with their head and feet near the ground. Four priests would be responsible for holding the subject down, and when they were secure, a fifth would come in with a flint knife to slit their chest and tear out their bleeding heart.

Another form of sacrifice resembles the tradition of gladiators in Ancient Rome. First, the victim had a huge stone tied to his leg to slow him down and limit his movement. He would then be given wooden weapons and be sent to battle Aztecs armed with regular weapons. It was an unfair fight to say the least, and it usually ended with the subject to be sacrificed bloody and wounded. He'd then be taken to a stone where the priests would perform a similar ceremony as with other sacrificial victims. When sacrifice was carried out in this manner, though, there was a possibility the victim could escape. If they were successful in fighting off the Aztec warriors, then they would be spared from sacrifice. However, this rarely happened given the disadvantageous position of the captive.

There were other ways of sacrificing people besides cutting out their heart. Women were sacrificed in the name of the goddess of the Earth, and this was done by chopping off their heads unsuspectingly while they danced. To make offerings to Tlaloc, the rain god, children were drowned, and sacrifices to the fire god were made by tossing people into a fire. To honor the god Xipe Totec, captives were tied up, shot with arrows, and then flayed. It was common practice to dress up those to be sacrificed in the image of the gods. This way, when blood was spilled, it was the blood of a god that was being offered, which is reflective of the way the Aztecs understood the creation of the Earth and all the living things that occupy it.

This commitment to human sacrifice had a considerable impact on the overall course of the Aztec Empire in a variety of different ways. First, it created the need for near constant warfare. The initial expansion of Aztec city-states created a large area of pacified communities. It would not have been sustainable for priests and rulers to draw from their own people for sacrificial subjects. But the need to quench the thirst of the gods remained, which is why most Aztec city-states were constantly at war. It was a source of great pride for the warriors who took part in these conflicts to be able to bring home captives to be sacrificed to the gods. Because of this, battles with Aztecs often looked rather strange. Many of the warriors were trying to kill as few people as possible, hoping instead to take prisoners back with them, as this would bring them glory and respect.

The other way in which the practice of sacrifice affected Aztec civilization was in how it made them appear to the Spaniards when they eventually made contact with the "New World" civilization. While the Spaniards were no saints, the image of people having their hearts ripped out from their chests while bent over a stone was one that was rather difficult for the newcomers to swallow. It was because of this that Spanish settlers came to view the Aztec gods as demons and the Aztec religion as something of evil. This instilled a responsibility in them to rid Mexico and its people from these evil ways.

While the idea of human sacrifice seems cruel to those of us armed with hindsight, it would be unwise to judge the whole of Aztec society based on this one practice. It was indeed violent, but it was also in line with their view of the world and what was needed to preserve its existence. Civilizations throughout time, up to and including the present day, have come up with diverse reasons and methods for killing large amounts of people at one time. We may look back and question the practices of the Aztec, but in doing so, it's important to also look at what is currently being done that might be viewed with the same level of shock and awe by someone arriving from the outside.

The Gods

It's clear that Aztec life was very much centered around religion. The central tenet of nearly all their military and civil expansion was to make sure the gods were satisfied and that the Earth had the blood it needed to continue existing. Furthermore, one of the principle duties of any sovereign, dignitary, or noble was to protect the local temple so that the gods could receive the worship that was owed to them.

Formal religions practice had two forms: human sacrifice and ceremonies that took place at the temples, and home worship. Most cities and towns had a patron god to which they were dedicated, and commoners would set up altars in their homes with idols of these gods so that they could worship them as they saw fit. One of the responsibilities women undertook as homemakers was to light incense, keep the house clean for the gods, and make sure the altar was sufficiently maintained, as well as gather offerings for anyone who had died in the previous four years.

But who exactly were these gods? How did the Aztecs understand the supernatural? As is evident from the various creation stories and reasons for sacrifice, the Aztecs had many gods, almost too many to count. It was believed that all gods descended from the aforementioned Lord and Lady of the Duality. But these gods were far removed from the actual administration of the Aztec world. Instead, the Lord and Lady of the Duality sat in the 13th heaven, creating gods, humans, and Earths as they saw fit.

Many of the Aztec gods are manifestations of other Aztec gods but in different forms, but many others stand on their own as separate deities. So, while it's impossible to compile a list of all the gods the Aztecs worshiped, it is possible to narrow the list down to a few main gods who would form the basis of the Aztec religion.

Quetzalcóatl

The story of Quetzalcóatl, one of the most important gods in Aztec religion, is vital to both the origin and the eventual demise of the Aztecs. The Aztecs traced their roots back to the Toltec people of Northern Mexico. In this culture, Quetzalcóatl was the priest-king of Tula, the Toltec capital. As ruler, Quetzalcóatl never offered human victims for sacrifice, choosing instead to spill the blood of snakes, birds, and butterflies. However, he was expelled from Tula by another Toltec god, Tezcatlipoca. When this happened, Quetzalcóatl began wandering to the south. After walking along the "divine water" (the Atlantic Ocean), Quetzalcóatl killed himself and emerged as the planet Venus (yet another connection between destruction and creation).

There is reason to believe that some version of these events actually happened. Early Toltec civilizations practiced theology and were focused on peaceful, non-violent living. However, the rulers responsible for disseminating this worldview were overthrown by a military aristocracy with a decidedly more militaristic perspective. Quetzalcóatl's travels to the southeast could refer to the invasion of Yucatan by the Itza, a tribe that was closely associated to the Toltecs.

One of the most significant connections between Quetzalcóatl and history, though, actually refers to the eventual downfall and destruction of the Aztec Empire. Legend said that Quetzalcóatl would return from his journey in a 1 Reed year (see the description of the calendar below). The year 1519 when Hernán Cortés and his team of conquistadors arrived on the coast of the Mexican Gulf was in fact a 1 Reed year. This led the ruler of the Aztecs at the time, Montezuma, to consider the arrival of the Spanish as something divine. He thought that the newcomers could be the incarnation of Quetzalcóatl, and this caused him to welcome them with open arms. This obviously proved to be a fatal mistake, as the Aztec Empire would crumble within just a few years after their first contact with the Spanish.

Quetzalcóatl represented many things to many different people. He was first conceived to be the god of vegetation, or of earth and water. In this sense, he was closely related to Tlaloc, the rain god. After a while, Quetzalcóatl's cult began to revere him as a heavenly body, linking him with the morning and evening star. During the peak of the Aztecs, Quetzalcóatl was the patron of priests, the inventor of the calendar and books, and the protector of goldsmiths and other craftsmen. And he was also closely related to the planet Venus. Quetzalcóatl is also credited with bringing life to this Earth. He was the one who traveled down into Mictlan to gather the bones of the dead. and used his blood to bring them to life, further emphasizing the role of blood and sacrifice in creating life.

Huitzilopochtli

Huitzilopochtli, or Uitzilopochtli, as it's sometimes spelled, is, together with Tlaloc, is one of the two principle deities in Aztec religion. Considering Huitzilopochtli was the god of the sun and war, it should not be a surprise that he occupied such a prominent position in Aztec religion. Aztecs believed that warriors would come back to Earth as hummingbirds, and this is why Huitzilopochtli is often depicted in paintings and sculptures as such.

Part of the reason why Huitzilopochtli occupies such a prominent role in Aztec religion is that he is credited for guiding the journey the Aztecs took from Aztlan, their traditional home in Northern Mexico, to the Valley of Mexico. Priests who went on this expedition carried statues and idols in the form of a hummingbird. It's said that at night Huitzilopochtli would appear and give orders to the travelers as to where they could find a suitable place to settle. It was Huitzilopochtli who informed them of the prickly pear cactus and eagle that would mark the spot of the Tenochtitlán settlement. Because of this, one of the first construction projects to take place in the new city was a shrine to Huitzilopochtli. This shrine would later turn into a temple and was enlarged by each ruler until 1487 when the emperor Ahuitzotl built another larger temple dedicated to the god.

While human sacrifice was seen as necessary to appease all of the gods, it took a prominent role in the Aztec worship of Huitzilopochtli. Since he was the sun god, and since suns require blood to exist, it was important that Huitzilopochtli received an adequate amount of blood each day. If he didn't, then the Aztecs believed they would be putting their entire world at risk of total annihilation. Since Aztecs believed people to be children of the sun, they saw it as their responsibility to provide the blood for Huitzilopochtli and the sun to continue to exist.

Another way you can see the importance of Huitzilopochtli in Aztec religion was in how they organized the clergy. Huitzilopochtli's high priest, along with that of Tlaloc the rain god, were together the head of the entire Aztec clergy. A full month of the ritual year calendar was dedicated just to Huitzilopochtli. These ceremonies would involve warriors dancing in front of the god's temple day and night. War prisoners and some slaves were bathed in a sacred spring before being sacrificed. Additionally, a giant image of Huitzilopochtli was made of corn, which was then killed ceremoniously, with the corn being divided among the priests and novices. If one consumed the body of Huitzilopochtli, then they were expected to serve him for at least one year, although most evidence suggests priests would extend this service obligation voluntarily.

Huitzilopochtli was far and away one of the most important gods in Aztec religion. His connection to war, and the direct link between his appeasement and human sacrifice helped to shape the way the Aztec world would develop and expand throughout the Valley of Mexico.

Tlaloc

Next to Huitzilopochtli in the divine hierarchy is Tlaloc, the Aztec rain god. The word Tlaloc translates from Nahuatl to mean "He Who Makes Things Sprout." Tlaloc was usually represented as a man with a peculiar mask, large eyes, and long fangs. Similar representations were used for the Maya rain god, Chac, suggesting a close relationship between the gods worshiped during the Maya and Aztec period.

The adoption of Tlaloc as not only the rain god but as one of the main gods of the Aztec pantheon represents the syncretistic nature of Aztec religion. Evidence suggests agricultural tribes in Mesoamerica had been worshiping Tlaloc for centuries. Living in more fertile lands, war was less of a priority for these people, meaning they found it more prudent to dedicate their spirituality to maximizing the yields given to them by Mother Earth. As the Aztecs moved into the

Valley of Mexico from the north, they brought with them their warlord gods, but they slowly adopted Tlaloc as an equal.

A full six months of the ritual calendar were dedicated to Tlaloc. During these months, people would engage in a wide array of ceremonies and rituals designed to honor Tlaloc and thank him for gifting them with rain and water to support life. Some of these rituals included bathing in the lake, dancing and singing using magic fog rattles (devices that made a loud rattling sound) to obtain rain, and making, killing, and eating idols made of amaranth paste.

Part of the reason Tlaloc was given so much attention was because he was both revered and feared. While he was responsible for bringing rains and for helping make the land bountiful, he could also be quite vengeful. Droughts, lightning, and hurricanes, among other natural disasters, were all attributed to Tlaloc. He could also send different types of rain depending on his mood, and he was also credited for certain diseases, such as dropsy and leprosy. Because Tlaloc could be both benevolent or ill-spirited, the Aztecs found it necessary to dedicate both time and energy to his worship, hoping that doing so would keep him happy and prevent him from unleashing his wrath on the Aztec people.

The high priest of Tlaloc joined the high priest of Huitzilopochtli to form the top of the Aztec clergy. Furthermore, the Teocalli (Great Temple) in Tenochtitlán had equal spaces dedicated to Huitzilopochtli and Tlaloc. This shared importance between Huitzilopochtli and Tlaloc helps us better understand how the Aztecs viewed the world. They understood their existence as something precious that was in constant danger. It was up to them to serve the gods enough to make sure they would allow them the time and space to continuing living on Earth.

Chalchihutlicue

As the wife of Tlaloc, Chalchihutlicue is one of the most important goddesses from the Aztec pantheon. Her name translates from

Nahuatl into "She Who Wears a Jade Skirt." Chalchihutlicue is the goddess of rivers, lakes, streams, and other freshwater bodies, and she was the ruler of the previous sun that existed before this one. It was during her reign that maize was first planted and cultivated; therefore, she is associated with this significant crop.

Coatlicue

Another important goddess is Coatlicue (Nahuatl: "Serpent Skirt"). She is the goddess of the Earth, and she is both the creator and destroyer. As the mother of both the gods and mortals, she occupies a position of prominence that is above most other deities. She is closer to the Lord and Lady of the Duality than most.

This dualism of creation and destruction defines the Aztec understanding and depiction of Coatlicue. Two fanged serpents are used to create her face, and her skirt is made up of woven serpents. Since she was responsible for nourishing both the gods and people, she had large, flabby breasts. She wears a necklace that is made up of hands, hearts, and a skull. These items were used because it was believed that Coatlicue fed off corpses—the Earth eats all that dies. Because of her position of power and dominance in Aztec religion, Coatlicue appears in many different forms, taking the form of both Cihuacóatl, the goddess of childbirth, and also Tlazoltéotl, the goddess of sexual impurity and wrong behavior.

Aztec gods are diverse and numerous. But they played a central role in shaping the way Aztecs lived their lives. Much of their day-to-day lives were spent trying to appease the gods, and one component of the empire's expansionist strategy was to acquire captives to be sacrificed. We may look back on it now and consider it crude, but this approach was in line with their worldview and belief system.

The Calendar

One important part of Aztec religion was their calendars. Yes, they had more than one. The calendars helped to organize agricultural practices and festivals, but they were also important in coordinating ceremonies and rituals throughout the year. The purpose of this calendar was to make sure that each god got their due worship.

The two calendars are quite different. The *xiuhpohualli*, or year count, is the agricultural calendar. It was based on the sun and the seasons, helping the Aztecs keep track of time and to make decisions about when to plant, water, harvest, etc. This calendar had been in use in Mesoamerica in some form or another since the time of the Maya.

This Aztec calendar is quite a bit different than the one we use today, although it has some similarities. For example, the Aztecs knew that one year lasted 365 days; they could figure this out by tracking the movement of the sun in the sky over the course of a year. However, the calendar is different in that it is divided into 18 months, with each month having 20 days. If you do the math, you'll realize that 18 multiplied by 20 is only 360. The other five days were left for the end of the year and were given no name. Aztecs considered these days to be very unlucky. They would spend the end of each year in temples making sacrifices to prevent anything bad from happening during these days of bad luck.

The *tonalpohualli*, or day count, is the ritual calendar of the Aztecs. There are only 260 days in this calendar, and each day has a corresponding number and sign. In total, there are 20 signs, with each one representing a different deity. These include:

- ○ Crocodile
- ○ Wind
- ○ House
- ○ Lizard
- ○ Serpent/snake
- ○ Death
- ○ Deer

- Rabbit
- Water
- Dog
- Monkey
- Grass
- Reed
- Jaguar
- Eagle
- Vulture
- Earthquake
- Flint
- Rain
- Flower

The first day of the *tonalpohualli* is 1 Crocodile. The numbers increase, lining up with their appropriate sign, until 13. It's unclear why this number was chosen. But after 13, the numbers reset. But since there are twenty signs, the next month does not start on 1 Crocodile. So the first month ends on 13 Grass and begins on 1 Reed. The second month then continues 13 days and ends on 13 Death, and the third month begins on 1 Deer and ends on 13 Rain, with the fourth month starting on 1 Flower. This cycle continues, and after 260 days, it returns to 1 Crocodile, and a new ritual year begins.

The two calendars run side by side, with the ritual calendar used as a way of keeping track of which god should be worshiped at a particular part of the year. The two calendars line up every 52 years. This moment marks the beginning of a new Aztec century. But the day when the two calendars coincided was one of great distress. Fifty-two years were considered to be one life cycle of the Earth, and at the end of each life cycle, it was within the gods' rights to take all that they had created and destroy it. Yet again we can see how the Aztec worldview was one dominated by the belief that this world could be destroyed by the gods at virtually any moment.

Another way in which the two calendars were tied together was in the naming of the years. Each year in the 365-day *xiuhpohualli* was named for the day on the *tonalpohualli* in which it ended. So, for example, the first year in the Aztec calendar is named 1 Reed because the first 365-day calendar ended on 1 Reed in the *tonalpohualli*. Since each year ends on a different day, each year has its own name. A year could be 12 Crocodile, 4 Grass, 5 Death, and so on. This helps to organize the years and to specify when events happened, although the mixing of the two certainly make it a challenge for outsiders to understand how the Aztecs measured time.

Much work has been done to try and completely recreate the Aztec calendar and to link it to other Mesoamerican calendar systems. In doing this, historians and archaeologists have been able to verify the dates of some of the more important events in Aztec history, specifically the birth and death dates of prominent rulers, the dates of conquest and military campaigns, and also the dates of interactions with the Spanish.

Chapter 8 – Sports

While much of Aztec life was occupied with worshiping the gods, working the land, and supplying tribute to the nobility, it was not all work. There was time for recreation, and an Aztec ballgame was one of the most popular activities.

This particular game, which is similar in rules and nature to volleyball or racquetball, was played throughout Mesoamerica. It took on special significance in the Aztec Empire largely because it was used both as an arena for human sacrifice, but also because it was connected to military training.

The game is played on a stone court and with a rubber ball. Players pass the ball back and forth using pretty much any body part they can, except their hands. , They could use their forearms, legs, hips, or head. There were many different variations of the game, with each town, village, or city having their own rules of play.

The significance of the game also varied greatly across Mesoamerica. It was frequently played in informal settings, with groups of villagers gathering and playing for fun. However, as the Aztecs advanced, large arenas were built where the game would be played in front of large crowds of people. These formal games were highly ritualistic, and some cultures even tied them into human sacrifice. The winners, losers, or both would be sacrificed to the gods after the game. It's for this reason that the Aztec ballgame, which is often referred to as *ulama* or *pok-a-tok* although its original name is still unknown, has been brandished as a bloody, brutal, and violent game.

But the truth is not all those who played the game did it for the purpose of sacrifice. That being said, though, the game has been known to cause serious injuries and even death. The large, heavy ball can inflict quite a bit of damage on a person's body when it strikes. When the Spanish arrived in Mexico, they were in awe of the game, but quickly labeled it as the devil's work when they witnessed some people using it as a means for human sacrifice.

Patolli is another sport that was popular among the Aztecs, although people had been playing it in Mesoamerica for centuries before. It's a board game of chance and skill. The table is in the shape of a cross and players need to move their stones across the table. Betting was common and in some places even integral to the game. People would gamble stones, gems, food, and sometimes even their own lives. Patolli is one of the oldest games in the world, and it's still played in many parts of Central America today.

Conclusion

In just a few hundred years, the Aztecs were able to advance themselves from a group of unwelcome hunters and gatherers to one of the largest and most advanced civilizations of the ancient world. Over time, a dedicated military tradition was combined with cultural hegemony and effective political institutions to form a fully-functional and expanding empire.

However, the Aztec civilization was far from perfect. Its despotic state required constant war, and the extractive system of taxes and tribute, as well as a heavily stratified society, meant that the Aztecs had many enemies when the Spanish arrived thirsty for blood and gold in 1519. In just a few short years after Cortés landed on the coast of the Mexican Gulf, the mighty Aztec Empire would fall and disappear into history books. But this did not happen before the Aztec people made a significant contribution to the historical and cultural development of Mesoamerica.

There are still many people alive today who can trace their heritage back to the Aztecs and the great empire forms a part of modern-Mexican identity. There's no telling what the Aztecs could have accomplished had the Spanish not arrived or had they had immunity to the many diseases that the invaders carried with them. Yet despite a sudden and untimely defeat, the Aztecs are still considered to be one of the greatest human civilizations to ever have formed.

Bibliography

Alcock et al. *The Aztec Empire and the Mesoamerican World System* in *Empires: Perspectives from Archaeology and History*, ed. Susan E. Alcock pp. 128–154. Cambridge University Press: New York.

Del Castillo, B. D. (1910). *The True History of the Conquest of New Spain* (Vol. 2)

Getty Research Institute (2010). *The Aztec Calendar Stone*. Los Angeles.

Murphy, J. (2015). *Gods and Goddesses of the Maya, Aztec and Inca.* Britannica Educational Publishing: New York

Smith, M. E. (2013). *The Aztecs*. John Wiley & Sons.

Soustelle, J. (1968). *Daily Life of the Aztecs*. Courier Corporation.

Villela, Khristaan D., and Mary Ellen Miller (eds.)

Whittington, E. Michael, ed. (2001) T*he Sport of Life and Death: The Mesoamerican Ballgame*. Thames and Hudson: New York.

Check out more books on Ancient History from Captivating History

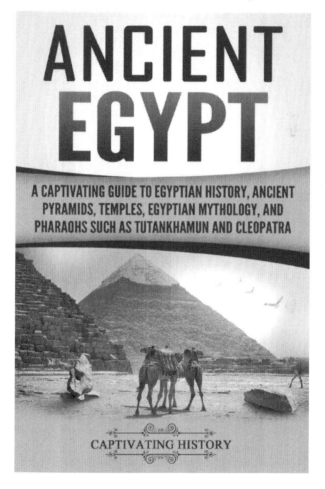

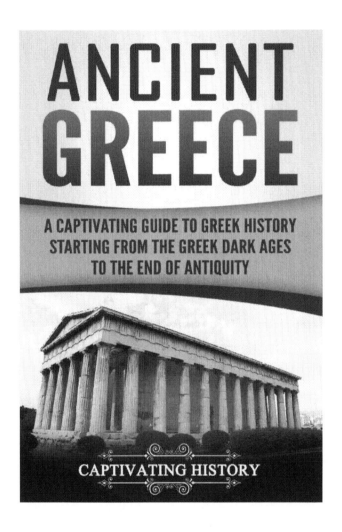

ANCIENT
GREECE

A CAPTIVATING GUIDE TO GREEK HISTORY
STARTING FROM THE GREEK DARK AGES
TO THE END OF ANTIQUITY

CAPTIVATING HISTORY

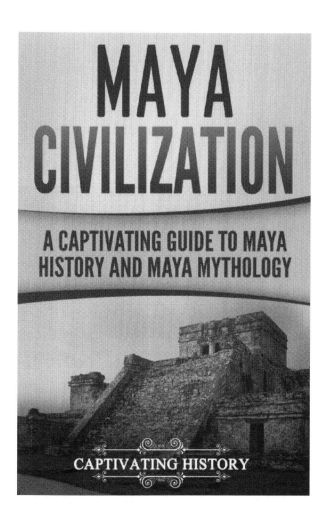

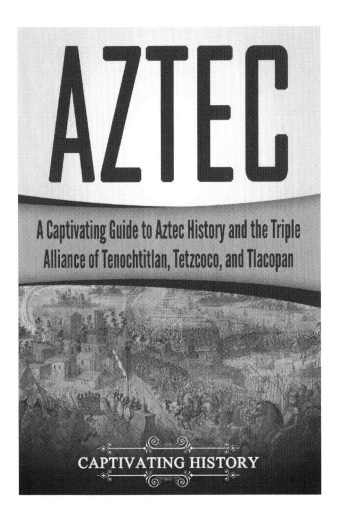

AZTEC

A Captivating Guide to Aztec History and the Triple
Alliance of Tenochtitlan, Tetzcoco, and Tlacopan

CAPTIVATING HISTORY

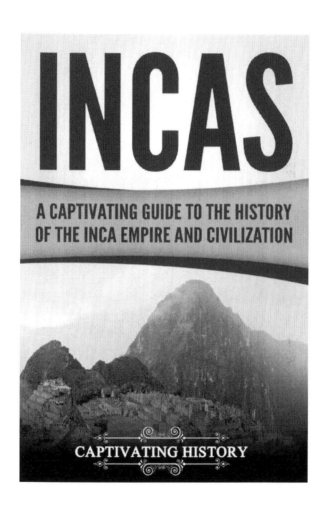

INCAS

A CAPTIVATING GUIDE TO THE HISTORY
OF THE INCA EMPIRE AND CIVILIZATION

CAPTIVATING HISTORY

HITTITES

A CAPTIVATING GUIDE TO THE ANCIENT
ANATOLIAN PEOPLE WHO ESTABLISHED THE
HITTITE EMPIRE IN ANCIENT MESOPOTAMIA

CAPTIVATING HISTORY

Free Bonus from Captivating History (Available for a Limited time)

Hi History Lovers!

Now you have a chance to join our exclusive history list so you can get your first history ebook for free as well as discounts and a potential to get more history books for free! Simply visit the link below to join.

Captivatinghistory.com/ebook

Also, make sure to follow us on:

Twitter: @Captivhistory

Facebook: Captivating History:@captivatinghistory

Printed in Great Britain
by Amazon